PROJECT

Copyright

Copyright © 2019 by Shanetta Oliver. All rights reserved.

Table of Contents

Making Money by Planning Cabaret Parties

Looking for a "side hustle" or a way to make extra money while having fun? Want to make an extra $500, $1000 or more a month planning parties for you and your friends?

Planning and hosting cabaret parties is one of the easiest and most fun ways to make extra money. You could host a parties once or more a month for consistent income, or every once in awhile to pay for bills, a new laptop or to finance a trip you've been dying to take.

This guide, was written by someone who has hosted many cabarets to make extra money, will show you how to plan your next cabaret from start to finish.

Basically, you're going to plan a party and charge people to attend.

Step-by-step instructions show how to set a budget, sell tickets, find live entertainment, secure vendors all the while making very good money.

What is a Cabaret?

Hosting a cabaret is a great way to mix fun and good times with making money. For those of you who are envisioning people donned in masks and elaborate costumes, then you are wrong.

Of course, cabarets were held in the 19th century and current ones are used to mimic them. However, cabarets can have any theme, but are usually any event held where people eat and drink in front of live entertainment.

During the Harlem Renaissance, African Americans held cabarets because they were often unable to entertain elsewhere. These functions involved people eating, drinking and dancing to live entertainment, usually a band.

Today, most cabarets held in the African American community resemble those from the Harlem Renaissance period.

Another form of events held during this time were what was known as "Rent Parties". During the 1920s and 1930s discriminatory practices in Harlem, New York called for extremely high rents for many African Americans.

Unfortunately, the pay for African Americans were also very low during this time. This combination often assured people would be short on their rent.

People would host rent parties in their homes and pass a hat around to collect money (or charge admission at the door) in return for food and entertainment.

Residents made enough to make their rent and guests usually left happy and entertained.

As time passed, the need for these rent parties became less necessary. Today, many people hold similar parties to make extra money to pay for necessary expenses or to make extra money.

Hop Mr. Bunny, Skip Mr. Bear,
If you don't dig this party you ain't no where!

* **A SOCIAL DANCE** *

—Given By—

DELORES and GLORIA

AT 66 WEST 133rd STREET, APT. 2N
New York City

Saturday evening, November 24th, 1956

—— *REFRESHMENTS* ——

35c. with Ticket   45c. without Ticket

Rent party cards from the Langston Hughes Papers (James Weldon Johnson Memorial Collection of African American Arts and Letters)

Picture of a rent party (date unknown) from Swamp River Newspaper

No matter if you want your cabaret to reflect the 19th century time period, the Harlem Renaissance or neither, you can still plan a cabaret and make money. You can even call it a party if you want.

Why Plan and Host a Party?

Cabarets are held all across the country, no matter what they are called. A cabaret, a party, a fish fry, etc., these events are planned to gather people for good times, but can also be a money making venture.

A person who may need help paying bills may have a cabaret to make ends meet. A non-profit organization may hold an event to fundraise money for their favorite cause. Or a small production company may hold these events to support their business.

Hosting a party, no matter what you call it, involves finding a venue, securing food and entertainment and charging admission.

Your profit margin is limitless and dependent on your creativity.

Your events can be as simple or as elaborate as you want.

Before You Start, Plan, Plan, and then Plan Some More.

In order for your event to be successful and for you to come out on the winning side, you will need to put some planning into your event in the beginning.

I suggest planning at least a month or two in advance. This takes off some pressure so you won't make careless mistakes that will cost you later.

The first or second time you hold your event may be stressful, but once you've held a few, you will become a pro.

I have seen many people hold cabarets that were complete successes, to those who tanked their events, therefore refusing to host another one ever again. Even I have goofed an event or two, but if you follow this guide, you will not make the same mistakes and will make good money for little effort.

The Guest List
Who You Want to Party With

Part of the planning process involves determining who you will invite to your cabaret. Will you invite friends, family, and acquaintances, or will you invite complete strangers?

Who you invite will determine the format of your event, but it will also determine your level of risk. So be careful.

First of all, I recommend gearing your event towards the 21 and over crowd. This is important, because you will likely serve alcohol at these events. Next, begin with your family and friends and encourage them to invite their family and friends. Later, as your experience and amount of money you can put into the event grows, you can broaden out to the general public.

Of course, if you already have a specific group to invite, such as women from your sorority, then it will be easy to figure out who to invite.

To hold a successful event, I recommend staying in your comfort zone. If you're in your early forties, I would warn against gearing your event to people in their early 20s. Remember your first event should be streamless.

Cabarets tend to do extremely well for people between the ages of 30 and 50. This is probably due to the fact that this group still wants to have a place to party, but are tired of the nightclub scene.

They are willing to pay money to be able to party in a fun and safe environment. This age group will be your money maker, especially at first.

Cabarets also work well in rural or more remote areas, however you may not be able to charge as much for a ticket that you would in the suburban areas.

Also, when you are deciding who to invite, make sure they you will be able to invite enough people to make a profit.

The Venue
Tell Me Where's the Party

Finding a place to hold your cabaret can either make or break your budget. Since, this will probably be your most expensive expense, you want to be sure to find a place that is accessible, has plenty of parking and doesn't cost a lot of money to reserve.

To make people want to party with you in the first place, you're going to have to find a place that is clean and safe part of town. No one wants to go to a place where they run the risk of getting robbed between their car and the door.

When looking for a place, look to local recreation centers and private halls of private organizations. They often rent their spaces to the general public.

Other places to consider:
- a large house (yours or someone else's)
- someone's large backyard (works great during warm weather)

- Elks Lodges
- Knights of Columbus Halls
- Local fire department halls
- Private rental halls

The Contract

When you have found a place you like, you will undoubtedly have to sign a contract and put down a deposit. Make sure you pay close attention to the contract. Failure to do so can destroy your event before you even hold it.

Read the fine print. Keep an eye on the occupancy rules. You don't want to plan for 200 people when the place can only hold 100. Having the fire marshal shut down your party will not be fun for anyone.

Other things to consider...What are the rules and regulations? Can you serve alcohol? Do you have to provide your own security? Can you charge admission for the event? Is the deposit in addition to the cost of the rental or will it be applied to the balance? If your questions are not answered in the contract, ask the person in charge. You don't want the surprise of having to obtain your own liability insurance if you didn't plan for it in the first place.

Pass on the venue if:

- the place is too expensive. You don't want to worry about selling enough tickets just to pay for the rental.
- It's in an unsafe or crime ridden area
- the contract has too many restrictions. Some places want to dissuade renters from holding cabaret-like events, especially if they charge admission.
- it doesn't allow alcohol. Unless this is a family-oriented event, adults will expect to drink.
- the venue requires you to use too many of their services, such as security and catering.

Money Saving Tip:

Avoid venues that book a lot of weddings or corporate events. These places are very expensive to rent for a cabaret.

Budget:
You'll Need it to Make Money

This is probably the most important thing to pay attention to when you are planning your next cabaret. Ignore it and your money will go right out the window. You want to have fun, but failure to follow a budget will eat into your profits. Instead of having cabarets to make money, you'll end up paying other people to party with you.

I once held a cabaret with my friends where we didn't even breathe the word budget in our conversations. As you can guess, our expenses went so out of control that not only did we not make any money, we ended up digging out of our own pockets to just break even. Don't be like us.

Costs to consider

Venue - Look around and compare prices. This will be your biggest expense, but it shouldn't cost more than a fourth of what you plan to bring in. For example, if you expect to bring in $2000, the place shouldn't cost more than $500 to rent.

Entertainment - Part of having a cabaret party is the live entertainment. You can have a live band, a comedian, or dancers as part of your live entertainment. Until you start making a lot of money and can charge a higher price for tickets, I would just stick with hiring a DJ.

A DJ will probably be your second highest expense for having a cabaret. When looking for a good one, ask for recommendations from family and friends. Speak to at least three and pick the best you can afford. If you know someone in your group that has a large repertoire of music, then you can ask them to play for you.

I would recommend not paying more than $400. Three hundred dollars or less is ideal, but again check your budget.

Just make sure the DJ knows the crowd he or she will be entertaining. Though you could provide a playlist, you would hate to hire someone who doesn't have the type of music selection your guests want to dance to. A bad DJ will stink up your whole event, so be careful.

Food - Are you going to serve food at your event? You don't have to, but I recommend providing at the very least finger foods. Not everyone will bring their own food, but if alcohol is being served, you want people to have something on their stomachs. You could serve cheese, crackers, fruits and veggies, but you could also serve chicken wingettes or bite-sized sandwiches.

You could serve what you want, but I would recommend some type of food to make people feel they got their money's worth. So if you're only serving potato chips, at least add some dip. Also, don't worry about having enough to feed everyone. Guesstimate how many people will be there and figure that over half will eat. Once it's gone, it's gone.

Setups - Weird name, I know, but you will need to provide ice, cups and soda for your guests. It's almost expected by people who regularly attend cabaret-like events.

Alcohol - You could provide alcohol, but I highly recommend against it. It's a budget killer. It will get too expensive too fast. People will drink more, just because of the fact it's free liquor.

You can get around it by indicating BYOB (bring your own bottle) on invites and people will bring alcohol with them. This is also expected. You could provide wine or maybe mixed frozen drinks to add something special to your event, but only if it can be done inexpensively.

Alcohol License - Expect to get one. Contact your local government agency to see how to apply for one and what the costs are. Any place that will serve alcohol will definitely require one. Make sure to check your contract first to see who is responsible for obtaining one. You don't want to have to pay twice if it is covered in the rental fee (not often the case though).

Security - One thing about having control over your guest list is the ability to determine your safety risk. Of course, things happen, but if you pick a crowd that is more mature or have familiarity with each other, you will not require a lot of security. However, if you have guests you don't know personally or if it will be a large crowd, I recommend obtaining security.

You could hire a security firm, but again this involves extra costs. You could also just ask your big and tall cousins to man the doors. Just give them a black shirt and a walkie talkie and they will look intimidating to anyone who may want to start a little mischief.

You could pay your security an hourly wage or just offer free admission. If you rotate individuals throughout the night, they will get the chance to party with everyone else after their shifts.

Invitations - You can make printed flyers and invitations, or just go by word of mouth. You could also send evites, which will cost you absolutely nothing. Of course, the higher the admission, the more effort your guests will expect.

Ticket Price
What Will Your Guests Pay to Party

How much will you charge for admission is a major decision to make when planning your cabaret. If you charge too much, most people won't come. However, if you charge too little, you won't make any money, therefore defeating the purpose of planning a cabaret party in the first place.

To determine how much to charge, you need to figure out first what your expenses will be. Add up the costs of the venue, the food, any licenses, etc. Add a little extra for surprises, but this is the amount you must have for the event to happen.

Next, figure out how many tickets you can reasonably sell. If you don't know many people, don't expect a huge crowd. Also, look at the occupancy of the venue. Don't expect to sell 200 tickets if the place only holds up to 100 people. It's no fun having your event shut down by the fire marshall.

Next, figure out how much profit you would like to make.

Finally, add your costs and potential profit and divide by the number of tickets you expect to sell. Your number will be the price of your ticket.

Example: Your costs will run about $800. You would like to make a profit of $1000.

$$\$800 + \$1000 = \$1800$$

You expect 150 people to buy tickets.

$$\$1800/\ 150\ people = \$12$$

This is the cost per ticket.

Now you could leave that number as is, decrease or increase it, but also decide what most people will pay. If most people pay $15 to attend cabarets, don't get greedy and charge $25. You won't have a successful event if you do.

Quick tip - People in the suburbs and cities expect to pay a little more than those living in rural areas.

Advertising
Tell Them and They Will Come

If this is your first cabaret, you could probably get started by word of mouth. Invite your friends and family and encourage them to invite their friends. Your event will be the talk of your group and everyone will be excited to attend.

To make sure everyone passes on the correct details about your event, I do suggest however, creating flyers and/or invitations. They can be as simple as you creating something on your computer and making copies.

This way people will have a reference to coordinate time and date and other particulars.

Other ways to advertise to your guests about your events:
   - Set up an event through your Facebook Page or create a unique Facebook Page for your event
   - Set up an event through Evite or Eventbrite
   - Create a website (if you're techy)

Unless you have held previous events and have the budget, do not spend a lot of money advertising your event.

Invitations - No matter if you are creating paper invitations or electronic ones, you must have specific information on it. This will prevent a lot of misunderstandings in the long run.

At the very least, each invitation should have:
- The name of the event. Think of something catchy. You want to show excitement from the very beginning.
- Date
- Time
- Location
- Cost of Ticket (also how and where to purchase them)
- Attire. Specify if it will be casual or people will need to dress up. If it's a themed event, specify that as well. You don't want people to arrive under or over dressed.
- Offerings. Let them know if there will be food or special entertainment.
- Age range. 21 and over to party is required if you're serving alcohol (also BYOB if they should bring their own liquor)
- Phone and email so they can get more information

Selling Tickets
Money, Money,
Money...Money

This is best part of the cabaret - selling tickets. In order to make money, you have to sell tickets. Refer to the section on Advertising as well as the Appendix for more ways to successfully sell tickets.

Depending on the number of people you are getting money from, you can just collect cash in person. Your goal should be to collect enough money to pay for your expenses at least two weeks before the event (or before the full balances are due).

Money, Money, Money...Money cont'd

You don't want to get close to the event stressing about paying for the place if you haven't even sold enough tickets. The only upfront costs you should have coming out of your pocket is the security deposit (though if you're creative enough, you could use the money from presales to pay for it).

You could also enlist the help of people you trust by encouraging them to sell tickets for you. If you go this route, make sure to have cash in hand before giving tickets.

  If you can't avoid this, make sure that when they bring you the money, they also return any unsold tickets.

You don't want to lose money with "free" tickets. You could give them an incentive of a free ticket if they sell 10 tickets for you. This will allow you to reach more people and sell more tickets.

Safety - Never put yourself in harms way. Don't carry large sums of money on your person. Deposit the money in a bank account as soon as possible or at the very least, put in a secure place such as a safe.

Many rental halls prevent you from collecting money for admission, so reread your contract. Most prevent you from collecting admission at the door. This is a safety risk, so make sure that people know that tickets will not be sold at the door in advance.

To safely sell more tickets, you may want to consider accepting payments online through PayPal, CashApp, or a service such as Eventbrite. You may even consider carrying around a card reader (such as Square) that will allow you to accept credit cards.

Safety
Fight for Your Right .... To Party. Not!

Holding a cabaret puts you in a place where you have the safety of your guests in your hands. Keeping everyone as safe as possible is your responsibility. Of course you can't prevent something bad from happening, but you can minimize your risk if you plan for something wrong happening in the beginning.

Do not sell tickets at the door. Even if your contract doesn't strictly prohibit you from collecting money at the door, I would suggest staying away from it. Unless you have security and a system in place, it's just not worth the hassle. If you must sell tickets or services such as photos at the event, have at least two people responsible for handling the money and keep it in a safe.

You could also consider getting a card reader and accept credit cards at your event. You can accept cards on your cell phone or your tablet effortlessly and there's no temptation for thieves, because the money will be deposited directly in your checking account in the next day or two.

Know Your Crowd - I believe that you should only invite people who are in your social circle for at least the first few cabarets you have.

Even if you don't know every person at your cabaret, these people were invited by people you have relationships with. The chance of something tragic happening decreases, because people are connected in some way, even if it's indirectly.

As you grow, you can broaden your reach to the general public because you know have the money needed to pay for increased security.

Market to an older, more mature and stable crowd. These people are less likely to fight or be hot-headed. Most of them have worked a long week and are looking for a way to unwind and relax. They don't have time for all the drama.

Though this doesn't guarantee something won't pop off, but you have lessened the likelihood it will.

Having to call the police will definitely shut the party down and disgruntled party goers will demand refunds. You will also get a bad reputation of having a bad crowd at your events and people may not want to come to any you host down the road.

The Day of the Event
Oh It's Party Time

If you have put all of the preparation into planning your event, the actual event should go pretty smoothly. Expect hiccups, but planning for the worse will help you to combat them pretty well.

Three Hours Before the Event - Unless you have superhuman powers you are going to need help setting up your event. You could enlist family and friends to help or you could hire people off of Craigslist to assist (however this is an additional cost). If you're not able to enter the hall just yet, you could use this time to pick up decorations, drinks and food.

Two Hours Before - Begin decorating the hall. Place tables and chairs in a good layout that allows room for getting around and dancing. Delegate duties to your helpers. If people are working in shifts, make sure they know where they are supposed to be and when.

One Hour Before - Make sure food, utensils, and

sodas are set up. You can wait until close to the time of the event before putting out the ice or food that may spoil. Make sure the DJ has arrived and has begun setting up. Set up a table at the entrance to collect tickets.

Quick tip: Use bracelets or hand stamps to make sure you can distinguish between people who have already purchased a ticket as they are coming and going.

Time of Event - Begin welcoming guests as they enter. Make sure the DJ has already started playing music and security is in place. Make an announcement as a good number of people have arrived, such as where the bathrooms are located or any other housekeeping issues that need to be addressed.

Use this time to thank everyone for buying a ticket and promise a good time.Make another announcement mid-way through the event repeating what you've already stated to catch the fashionably late crowd up.

An Hour Before the Party is to End - Make an announcement that the party will end at the specified time. This allows people the opportunity to wind down and begin sobering up if they have been drinking. Begin cleaning up bottles and trash, so you won't have a lot to do at the end of the cabaret. Award raffle ticket winners at this time if you haven't already.

Thank guests for coming and for supporting your event. If you're planning another event, let them know to expect more information about it later.

At the End of the Party - Have the DJ turn off the music. This is a universal signal that the party has stopped. It will also motivate people to begin packing up. Have your clean up crew go around cleaning up by picking up trash and rearranging the tables and chairs back to how you found it.

Leave on-time, return the keys and do anything to ensure you receive your security deposit back.

Go home, relax and count your money.

You have just held your first cabaret and hopefully everything went well.

Extra, Extra...
Tools to Help You to Run a Profitable Side Business

On the next few pages, I have provided a few tools to help you while planning your money-making cabaret.

If you have followed the steps in this guide, you will have made money from your very first event. If not, you did something wrong. Either you paid too much for the hall or the DJ or you charged too little for tickets.

I have created a few resources that help me when I plan my events that should be helpful to you and put money in your pocket. Hopefully these tips will help you to avoid making expensive mistakes in the process.

Appendix
Planning and Budget
Worksheets to Plan a
Profitable Cabaret

Pre-Planning Worksheet

Before you start planning your cabaret, ask yourself the following questions.

1. **Who will I invite?** *Do the guests have anything in common (are they part of the same group or community)? What are their ages? Where do they live?*

2. **How much money do I want to make?** *Do I want to make enough to cover bills or do I want to make a full-time income from hosting cabarets?*

3. **How will I sell tickets?** *Will I sell tickets face-to-face, call on others to help sell, or sell them online?*

4. **Where do I want to have the cabaret?** *Will I need to rent space?*

5. **What is the theme of this event?** *Is it a birthday or holiday celebration?*

Budget

Costs_____

Total Amount Due_____

Venue _____ _____/_____/_____

Security Deposit _____ Due _____/_____/___

Alcohol License Application _____

Insurance (if required) _____

Entertainment

DJ _____

Other _____

Food, Ice, Soda, etc. _____

Printing (for tickets) _____

Decorations _____ **Paper Products** _____

Security or other Personnel Fees _____

Miscellaneous _____

Total Anticipated Costs _____

Profitability Worksheet

I would like to make $_____
from this cabaret AFTER expenses are
paid. This is my profit (the goal is to
ALWAYS have a profit).

My expenses will cost me $_____
(get this amount from your Budget
worksheet).

_____ + _____ = _____
    Profit   Expenses   Goal

Your **goal** is what you must earn from
holding this cabaret. This is the amount
you expect to make AFTER everything is
paid for.. If you are in the negative, go
redo your budget or increase your ticket
prices.

If you're not making money, you shouldn't
have a cabaret.

Point blank.

Fun Themes

The fun part of hosting your own cabaret is that you can make it what you want. If you want to hold a traditional event, go right ahead. As you begin to become more comfortable hosting these cabarets, you may want to put a spin on them. Themed events help with decorating and costume ideas, without a lot of effort. Not many people need a reason to party, but if they do - give it to them.

Here are a Few Ideas

- Holiday (New Year's, Valentine's, St. Patrick's, Halloween and Christmas are great holidays to schedule your event and usually come with easy color schemes to decorate to)
- Mardis Gras (pass out beads and have people to wear masks)
- Singles Mixer (invite only single women and men)
- Greek Party (have people come to represent their sorority or fraternity)
- Mother's Day Brunch
- Talent Show for Children and Teens (charge parents and family and use money for awards)
- Oldies but Goodies
- Decade Themed (70s, 80s, 90s, etc.)

You are only restricted to your level of creativity

Tools You Can Use

Here are a few tools that can help you when planning for your first (or next) party.

Eventbrite - to sell tickets online

Canva - (to design invitations and tickets)

Trello - to keep organized and complete tasks

Busyconf- keep the planning simple

Appmyday- this app will help you keep a uniformed look for your event news and updates

Party Supplies (Most of these you can find them at your local party store or Amazon.com).

Tickets - if you like to buy tickets instead of making them

Glowsticks - because why not? Not just for the New Year's Eve.

Party Tub - great for holding ice and/or beverage bottles

Wristbands - great way to keep track of people who have already paid

Cashbox - keep your money safe

Glitter Photo Backdrop- save the memories with photos.

Can't click on the links? If this is a printed version, you may find resources over at:
https://wp.me/P7y6lW-17N

Example Scenario

Still not sure you can host your own event just yet? Don't worry, I got you covered.

Over the next few pages I will show you a process for planning an event in a local area.

Let's say I decided to rent out a fire hall in Northern Virginia (Washington DC suburb) area.

Here are my preliminary costs (some are subject to change and can be altered depending on budget).

Fixed Costs

Hall Rental - $850 (due within 14 days of the event). 8-hour rental including set-up, event, and clean up time.

Deposit - $350 (due at the time of signing the contract).

Capacity - 140 people with tables and chairs (300 people with chairs)

Alcohol (banquet) license for 1 day - $55

Variable Costs

Food and Drinks - $150

DJ - $400

Flyer/Ticket Printing - $50

Upfront Total Costs: $1,855

Even though the venue can hold 140 people with tables and chairs, I plan to sell about 120 tickets. This will allow me to give a few extra tickets away for free and account for not selling enough tickets.

In order to break even, I will need to price my tickets AT LEAST $15 ($1,855 divided by 120 = $15.46).

However, my goal is to make money not break even, so if I increase ticket prices to $20, I can make about $2400 or $545 profit.

I can even charge $25 or $30 per ticket, because the event will be held within a metropolitan area and people are able and willing to pay more for entertainment.

However, I will keep it at $20 for this example.

I won't need security, because it's within a fire hall and there are firefighters on duty nearby and I expect to know most of the people I'm partying with.

Keeping the party within your social circle keeps things safe.

In addition, I expect to receive my entire security deposit of $350 back at the conclusion of the event.

Food

I will serve potato chips, pretzels, chicken wingettes, and a veggie/fruit platter. There's no need to worry about feeding 140 people, because some people will come with food or won't eat at all.

I will have several 2-liter sodas, water, and ice for guests. I will make sure to have more than enough.

(You can budget what you will when it comes to food and drinks. You may decided not to even bother with cooked or prepared food).

If I stay within budget, I should profit at least $500 (but up to $900 including return of deposit).

Not bad for a little preparation and fun night, huh?

Ways to Save More Money

I just showed you a rough example, however you can save money when it comes to the variable costs. These savings can be added into your profit margin and making over a thousand dollars is possible.

- Get family and friends to donate food and drinks, paper plates, and plasticware.
- Provide only chips and drinks (no cooked or prepared food)
- Fogo the live entertainment and play from your own device (make sure there's a good sound system)
- Get volunteers to provide the entertainment
- Find a cheaper venue
- Know someone with a large home? Offer to give to give them a few dollars to hold the event there.
- Partner with someone you trust. You'll split the upfront costs and responsibility. May cut into your profit a bit, however this widens your social circle and increases the likelihood of selling more tickets.

Your goal is to spend as little as humanly possible while allowing guests to still have a good time.

You want your guests to have a memorable experience, however you want to make money too.

Ways to Make More Money

Making more money from your parties will become easier as you start hosting more. You want to make as much as you can, because unless you're having a party every weekend, you're going to want each one to count. As you become more confident, you'll find creative ways to add more profit to your side hustle.

Here are a few ways to make more money...

- Increase your ticket price
- Invite more people
- Sell tickets at staggered times (in the example above, I have the place for about 7 hours + 1 hour for set up and clean-up, however most people won't stay that long. As long as I don't go over the 140 occupancy at any given time, I can sell more tickets. For example, if 50 people party from 8 to 10 PM, then that leaves room for 50 additional people to party from 10 PM to 12 AM).
- Sell ventor tables, if it fits with the theme of your party and guests.
- Sell products and services at the party such as t-shirts and photos.

Always look for ways to increase your bottom line. You want your guests to have a memorable experience, however you want to make money too.

Real Life Examples

Still not convinced people are having Cabaret parties throughout the country?

I've included a few examples I've found just cruising the internet. These events follow the same premise I describe, but each are unique in their own way.

The goal is to do it your way, have fun, and make money.

Flyer Examples

Each of these belong to their respective owners.

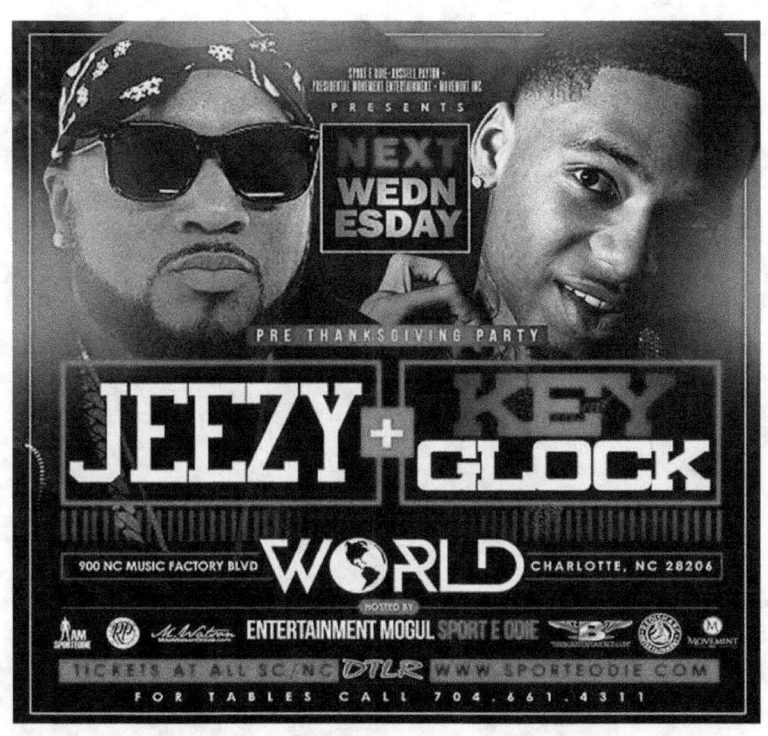

Flyer Examples

Each of these belong to their respective owners.

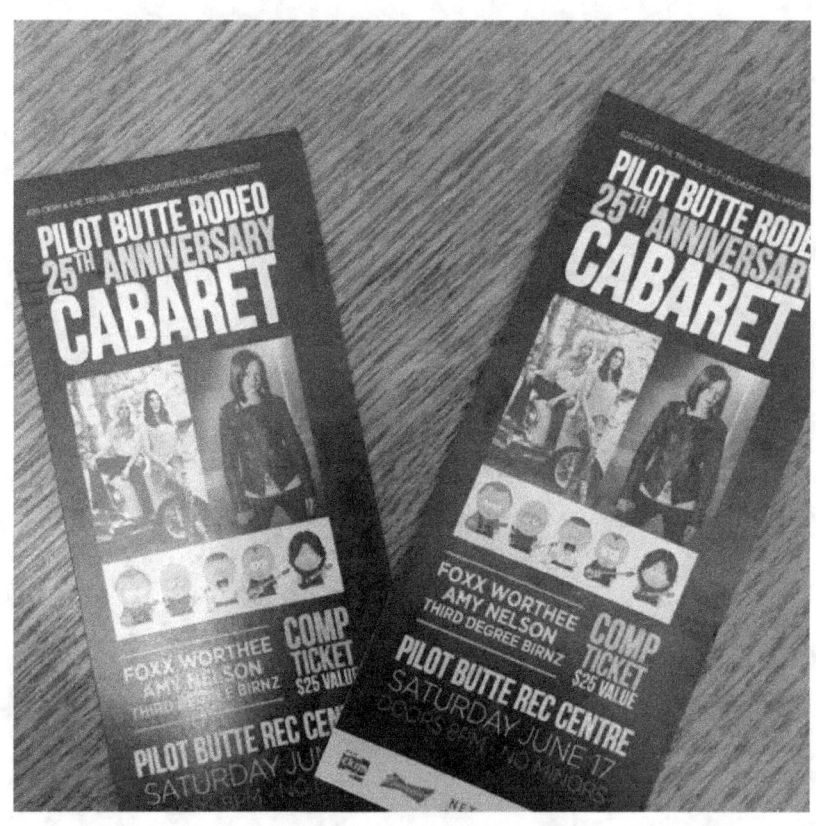

the miners foundry and paul emery present
newyears eve
MOJO GREEN
WHEE THE PEOPLE
funk party
FULL BAR
FOOD
MIDNIGHT CHAMPAGNE
MINERS FOUNDRY
CULTURAL CENTER
doors 8:00pm miners foundry 325 spring street nevada city
$25 general $30 reserved cabaret seating
minersfoundry.org 530.265.5040
december thirtyone

Ticket Examples

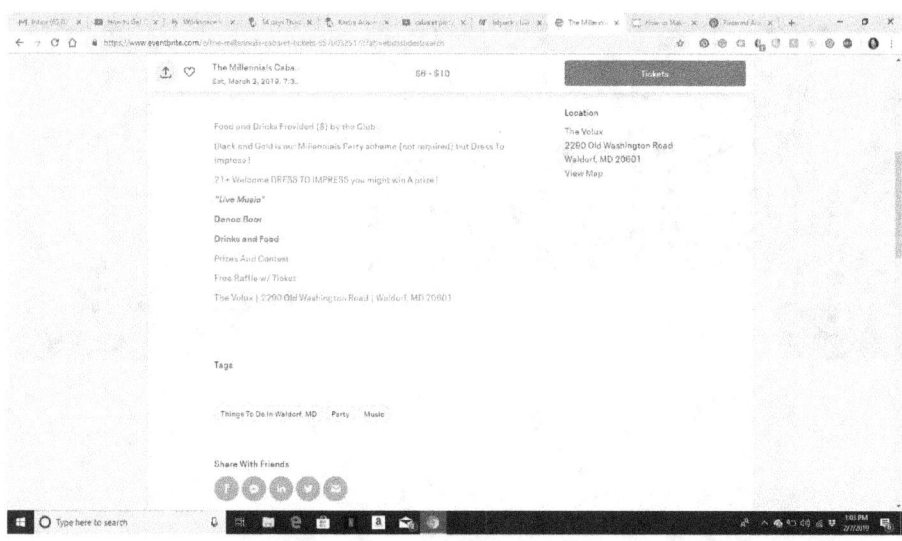

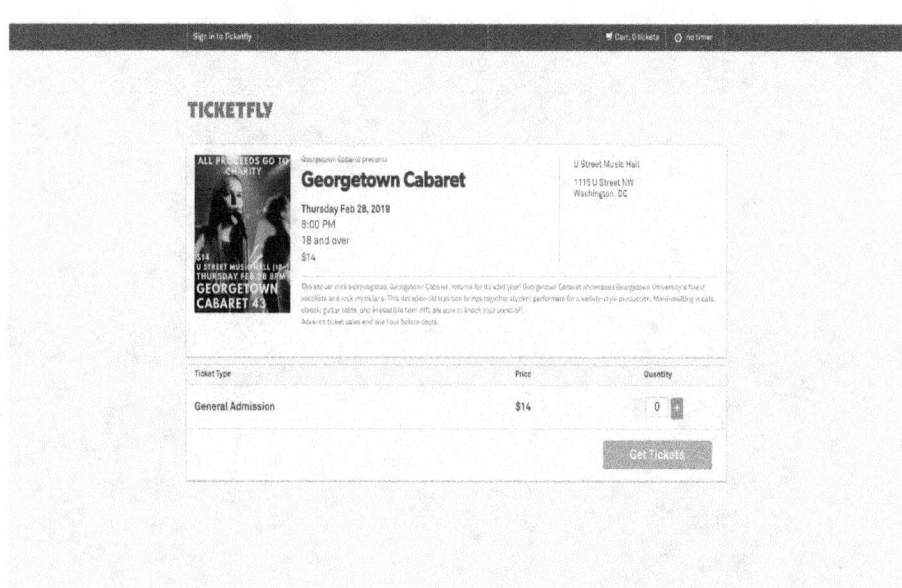

MAR
02

The Millennials Cabaret

by Jay "Iman" Wise

$8 - $10

⬆ ♡

Tickets

Description

Its 2019 its time to admit "We are the Party " ! This is It OUR first Millennials Cabaret @ The Volux (used to be SkyBar) March 2nd by Us for Us ! We have Special Guest Hosts, Dj Oneway Ricky ,Dj Clutch , Contest , Raffle Drawings and Special Performances for a LIT night

Food and Drinks Provided ($) by the Club .

Black and Gold is our Millennials Party scheme (not required) but Dress To Impress !

21+ Welcome DRESS TO IMPRESS you might win A prize !

"Live Music"

Date And Time

Sat, March 2, 2019
7:30 PM – 11:00 PM EST
Add to Calendar

Location

The Volux
2290 Old Washington Road
Waldorf, MD 20601
View Map

Smut Slam DC: Birthday Cabaret

Smut Slam DC
Wednesday, February 20, 2019 from 7:00 PM to 11:00 PM (EST)
Washington, DC

Ticket Information

TICKET TYPE	SALES END	PRICE	FEE	QUANTITY
Pre-sale (includes a raffle ticket!)	Feb 20, 2019	$15.00	$2.95	Sold Out

Enter promotions' code

Save This Event

Oh no! You've just missed the cutoff for online sales. You can buy tickets at the door for $20, but we recommend arriving early so you're sure to get in. We start releasing door sales at 7pm. (May we recommend grabbing food in the Lounge beforehand?)

Share Smut Slam DC: Birthday Cabaret
✉ Email 📷 Share 🐦 Tweet 👍 Like Be the first of your friends to like this

Event Details

Presale tickets for this show have sold out. But do not despair! We are holding tickets at the door for all you procrastinating lovelies. Door sales will begin at 7pm, at the venue. You can pay cash or use venmo. And as a heads up, the line usually begins forming by 6:30. Good luck!!
This show will have ASL interpretation
Smut Slam DC: Birthday Cabaret
We're throwing a fabulously frisky fete to celebrate our third birthday, and you're on the VIP (very intimate Perverts) guest list! This is Smut Slam like you've never seen it before: The Smut Slam Cabaret, where we're bursting up the stage with an unforgettable mix of some of the District's hottest talent. Salacious storytellers trade off with exhibitionist entertainment in

When & Where

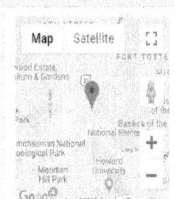

Ten Tigers Parlour
3813 Georgia Avenue Northwest
Washington, DC 20011

Wednesday, February 20, 2019 from 7:00 PM to 11:00 PM (EST)

Thank You

I hope you enjoyed the tips I shared with you in the book as well as learned a new (and fun) way to make money.

If you follow the steps I laid out in this book, you should have a fairly successful (i.e. profitable) party.

Thank you for reading this book. I wish you much success.

Please send me a message over at ShanettaOliver.com and let me know how your first event went and how much money you made!

www.ingramcontent.com/pod-product-compliance
Lightning Source LLC
Chambersburg PA
CBHW071243220526
45468CB00002B/982